SandCastle

Keeping the Peace

Working Together

Pam Scheunemann

Consulting Editor, Diane Craig, M.A./Reading Specialist

ABDO
Publishing Company

Published by ABDO Publishing Company, 4940 Viking Drive, Edina, Minnesota 55435.

Printed in the United States.

Credits
Edited by: Pam Price
Curriculum Coordinator: Nancy Tuminelly
Cover and Interior Design and Production: Mighty Media
Photo Credits: BananaStock Ltd., Brand X Pictures, Image Source, PhotoDisc, Stockbyte

Library of Congress Cataloging-in-Publication Data

Scheunemann, Pam, 1955-
        Working together / Pam Scheunemann.
            p. cm. -- (Keeping the peace)
        Includes index.
        Summary: Describes everyday actions, such as helping with homework, sharing chores, and playing on a team, that demonstrate the benefits of cooperation.
        ISBN 1-59197-562-X
        1. Cooperation--Juvenile literature. 2. Peace--Juvenile literature. [1. Cooperativeness. 2. Peace.] I. Title.

HD2963.S33 2004
646.7'6--dc22
                                                                            2003057782

SandCastle™ books are created by a professional team of educators, reading specialists, and content developers around five essential components that include phonemic awareness, phonics, vocabulary, text comprehension, and fluency. All books are written, reviewed, and leveled for guided reading, early intervention reading, and Accelerated Reader® programs and designed for use in shared, guided, and independent reading and writing activities to support a balanced approach to literacy instruction.

Let Us Know

After reading the book, SandCastle would like you to tell us your stories about reading. What is your favorite page? Was there something hard that you needed help with? Share the ups and downs of learning to read. We want to hear from you! To get posted on the ABDO Publishing Company Web site, send us e-mail at:

sandcastle@abdopub.com

SandCastle Level: Transitional

Working together keeps the peace.

Sue, Carrie, and Lindsay work together to decorate a cake.

There are many ways people can work together.

Steve and Lisa take turns walking their dog.

Lisa walks Spot while Steve is at his piano lesson.

Andy and Deb have chores to do at home.

The chores get done faster if they work together.

Dana helps her mom in the garden.

Their family enjoys the vegetables that they grow together.

Liz likes playing on the soccer team.

The best way to score a goal is by working together.

Everyone has different ideas about how to do something.

Corey and Nell work together to create an art project.

Laura needs help with her homework.

Her friend Amy is happy to work with her on her reading.

Sometimes a group needs to raise money for a project.

Ron and his friends work together to raise money for a new skateboard park.

Pete and his youth
group help build
a house for a family.

Good things can
happen when people
work together.

What can you do to keep the peace?

Glossary

chore. a regular job or task, like cleaning your room

create. to make something

different. not alike

family. a group of people related to one another

money. coins and bills that you use to buy things

together. joined into one group or place

About SandCastle™

A professional team of educators, reading specialists, and content developers created the SandCastle™ series to support young readers as they develop reading skills and strategies and increase their general knowledge. The SandCastle™ series has four levels that correspond to early literacy development in young children. The levels are provided to help teachers and parents select the appropriate books for young readers.

Emerging Readers
(no flags)

Beginning Readers
(1 flag)

Transitional Readers
(2 flags)

Fluent Readers
(3 flags)

These levels are meant only as a guide. All levels are subject to change.

To see a complete list of SandCastle™ books and other nonfiction titles from ABDO Publishing Company, visit **www.abdopub.com** or contact us at:

4940 Viking Drive, Edina, Minnesota 55435 • 1-800-800-1312 • fax: 1-952-831-1632